T ★ H ★ E
ZEBRA-RIDING COWBOY

A FOLK SONG FROM THE OLD WEST

Collected by Angela Shelf Medearis
Illustrated by María Cristina Brusca

HENRY HOLT AND COMPANY ★ NEW YORK

Come listen to my story, come listen to my song,
About a handsome stranger and a horse called Zebra Dun.

We were camped on the plains at the head of the Cimarron,
When along came a stranger who stopped to argue some.

He looked so very foolish, we began to look around;
We thought he was a greenhorn just escaped from town.

Such an educated fellow, his thoughts just came in herds;
He astonished all the cowboys with jaw-breaking words.

He just kept on talking till he made all the cowboys sick,
And they began to think to see how they could play a trick.

He said he'd lost his job out on the Santa Fe,
Was bound across the plains to strike the Seven D.

We asked him how it happened; he said,
   "Trouble with the boss,"
And asked if he could borrow a fat saddle horse.

This tickled all the boys to death, they laughed
     up their sleeves:
"We'll lend you a fine horse, as fat as you please."

Shorty grabbed a lariat and roped the Zebra Dun.
We gave him to the stranger and waited for the fun.

Old Dunny was an outlaw; he'd grown so awfully wild
That he could paw the moon down and jump for a mile.

But Dunny stood there still, just as if he didn't know,
Until we had him saddled, all ready to go.

When the stranger hit the saddle, old Dunny quit the earth
And traveled right straight upward for all that he was worth,

Pitching, squealing, screaming, and throwing wall-eyed fits,

His hind feet perpendicular, his front feet in the bits.

We could see the tops of mountains under Dunny's
        every jump,
But the stranger seemed to grow there,
        just like a camel's hump.

The stranger sat upon him and curled his black mustache
Like a summer boarder waiting for the hash.

He thumped him on the shoulders,
    and he spurred him when he whirled;
He showed all those cowboys
    who was top man in the world.

And when he had dismounted and stood there on the ground,
We knew he was a cowboy and not a gent from town.

The boss was standing close by, watching all the show;
He walked up to the stranger and said he needn't go:
"If you can use a lasso like you rode the Zebra Dun,
You're the man I've been looking for since the year One."

He spent the season with us, and the cowboys all agreed
There was nothing that he couldn't do,
    save stopping a stampede.

So there's one thing and a sure thing I've learned
since I've been born,
Every educated fellow's not a plumb greenhorn.

Afterword

One summer afternoon, my nephew Kenneth Ray came over for a visit. Somehow, we got into a conversation about cowboys.

"There weren't any black cowboys," argued Kenneth Ray.

I knew that he was wrong, but I did not have any proof at hand. Determined not to lose an argument to a five-year-old, I went to the library where I got a few books with pictures of African-American cowboys such as Bose Ikard, One-Horse Charlie, Bill Pickett, and Nat "Dead-Eye Dick" Love to show to Kenneth Ray. I also found a book of cowboy songs that contained the wonderful song on which this book is based.

Frontier cowboys traveled day after day with few comforts. The songs they sang helped pass the time and the music also soothed the cows and horses when they got restless. "The Zebra-Riding Cowboy," also known as "The Zebra Dun," was written between 1870 and 1890; the songwriter is unknown. The song is about a horse with zebralike stripes owned by the Z-Bar Ranch. Like other popular cowboy songs of that time, "The Zebra Dun" was passed from one singer to another, each cowboy changing the song a bit to fit his own style.

The "educated fellow" in this song has never been identified, but he might have been someone like Houston Bassett, an African-American who grew up tending horses, cows, and crops on his father's farm in Grimes County, Texas. He started school at the age of ten. Later he attended Straight College in Louisiana, and Fisk University in Tennessee. In 1886 Bassett

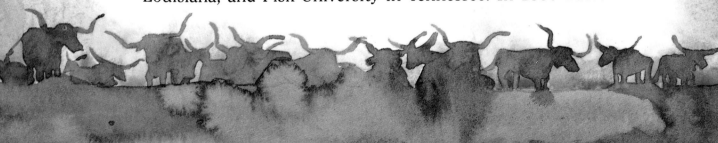

was elected as a representative to the Texas legislature. The educated fellow might also have been one of the African-American men who learned to read and write while serving in the Union Army during the Civil War. When the war was over, five thousand to eight thousand African-American veterans became cowboys, wranglers, cooks, and trail bosses.

Though the hero of this song could have been African-American as I imagined him, he also could have been white or Hispanic. Mexican vaqueros were the first cowboys in North America, and they were also an important part of the frontier life after the Civil War. Vaqueros introduced to the Old West many cowboy techniques and equipment used today, such as cattle branding, rodeos, and the lariat. Even the way cowboys dressed was influenced by the vaqueros. High-heeled boots, chaps, spurs, and the ten-gallon hat were all first worn by Mexican vaqueros.

Many books, movies, and television programs fail to include Mexican and African-American cowboys when they portray life in the Old West. María Cristina Brusca and I have attempted to correct this oversight in this book.

Angela Shelf Medearis

For my cowboys, Kenneth Ray, Michael, and Cameron,
with love from their auntie —A. S. M.

For Georgia Bailey Dalto, a cowgirl from Maine —M. C. B.

First edition
Published by Henry Holt and Company, Inc.,
115 West 18th Street, New York, New York 10011.
Published simultaneously in Canada by Fitzhenry and Whiteside Ltd.,
195 Allstate Parkway, Markham, Ontario L3R 4T8.

Library of Congress Cataloging-in-Publication Data
Medearis, Angela Shelf.
The zebra-riding cowboy: a folk song from the Old West / collected
by Angela Shelf Medearis; illustrated by María Cristina Brusca.
Summary: In this Western folk song, an educated fellow mistaken
for a greenhorn proves his cowboy ability by riding a wild horse.
Includes a discussion of Afro-American and Hispanic cowboys
in the nineteenth century.
ISBN 0-8050-1712-7
1. Children's songs—Texts. [1. Cowboys—Songs and music.
2. West (U.S.)—Songs and music. 3. Folk songs—United States.]
I. Brusca, María Cristina, ill. II. Title
PZ8.3.M551155Ze 1992
782.42162'13078—dc20   91-27941

Henry Holt books are available at special discounts
for bulk purchases for sales promotions, premiums,
fund-raising, or educational use. Special editions
or book excerpts can also be created to specification.

Printed in Mexico on acid-free paper. ∞

Designed by Victoria Hartman
10 9 8 7 6 5 4 3 2 1